Heart Thoughts: Real Storie
© 2025 by Cheri Taylor Min
Printed August 2025. All Ri
be reproduced or transmitte
or mechanical, including photocopying and recording, or by any
information storage or retrieval system, except as may be expressly
permitted inwriting by the publisher. Permission requests should be
addressed in writing via email to Lily of the Valley Publishing, Inc.

Requests may be sent to: publishing@mylilyofthevalley.org

ISBN: 979-8-9929634-5-8 (paperback)

Copyright Disclaimer under Section 107 of the Copyright Act (1976): Allowance is made for fair use for purposes such as criticism, comment, news reporting, teaching, and research. Fair use is a use permitted by copyright statute that might otherwise be infringing. Non-profit, educational, or personal use tips the balance in favor of fair use. Scripture quotations marked (KJV) are taken from the Holy Bible, King James Version, Cambridge, 1769, which is public domain. All rights reserved. Scripture quotations marked (NIV) are taken from the Holy Bible New International Version, NIV. Copyright 1973, 1978, 1984 by Biblica, Inc. All rights reserved. www.zondervan.com

Scripture quotations marked (NKJV) taken from the New King James Version. Copyright 1982 by Thomas Nelson, Inc. All rights reserved.

This book is designed to provide accurate and authoritative information with regard to the subject matter covered. This information is given with the understanding that neither the author nor Lily of the Valley Publishing, Inc. is engaged in rendering legal, professional advice.

Interior Design by Lily of the Valley Publishing Services
Cover Design by SumwhatSouth Creative
www.sumwhatsouth.com

Lily of the Valley Publishing, Inc.
Santa Claus, Indiana 47579 USA
| www.mylilyofthevalley.org |

Contents

Foreword	
Chickens	1
Clay Huff Christmas	3
Crying Out to God	5
Encouragement	7
Flip Phone Hubby	8
Answered Prayer Through a Simple Song	10
My Greatest Love	13
Friendship	15
Mirror, Mirror	17
Open Bible	19
Piano Recital	21
Restoration	23
Seneca Rock	25
Testimony Time	28
The Man on the Street	30
Watchful Eye	32
Where is Peace	34
Angels Unaware	36
Broken Pastor	38
Decaf Please	41
De	43
Forgiving Her	45
Friendship Baptist Church: He is Enough	47
God, Are You Proud of Me?	49
God's Great Love	51
Grandma	53
Grandpa Tony	56
Happy Birthday	58
Just Passing Through	60
No More Excuses	63
Speed It Up	65
The Blessings of Brokenness	67
The T-Shirt	69
Influence	71
My Greatest Fear	73
Hold Me	75
Audience of One	77

Lift Up Those Shackled Arms	79
No Mic Needed	81
The Power of Your Words	83
VBS Bus Driver	85
The Toothbrush	87
Snowstorm of the Year	89
Final Thoughts from My Heart	91

Foreword

When I think of Cheri Taylor, I think of many things. All great, by the way. Actually, "Heart" and "Thoughts" are two of the things that come to mind. She has a heart for ministry. She communicates the message of the Gospel not only through song, but also through women's ministry, and simply by being Cheri.

What I mean by that is that no matter where she is or what she is doing, ministry is always...ALWAYS...on her mind! We should all aspire to have that kind of heart. And, she is a virtual "thought machine." Her mind never shuts down. I get texts, emails, and calls from her nearly 24 hours a day. And, it's never about frivolous things. As I just stated, her thoughts are the same when speaking of the heart of who she is. Her thoughts are always...ALWAYS...on ministry!

May we all have a heart like Cheri Taylor. May we all have thoughts like Cheri Taylor. From the hearts of everyone in the Butler family, we send our love to Cheri and Greg Taylor! Enjoy her heart and be blessed by her thoughts. ~ Les Butler

Chickens

"Seek ye first the Kingdom of God..."- Matthew 6:33

My earliest memory of growing up on a farm is the chickens. Oh, how I hated those things! They always nipped at my heels as I helped my mother gather eggs. Keep in mind, this was not a quaint little chicken farm for the sake of having a few eggs. We had about two thousand at any given time, and I did NOT like them! Now, don't go rolling your eyes as if I were a rebellious child who didn't want to help. I was only three when my father began his farming adventure! The rebellious farmer in *me* came later, but that's another story, for another time.

The chickens, however, were only part of my father's dream. With barely two pennies to rub together, my young parents successfully purchased a bit of ground where my dad began crop farming while, at the same time, he was always looking ahead for another opportunity.

Cue in the pigs...I didn't like them either! Especially as the older me would be told of the early morning wake-up calls to help load and take them to market. Other adventures with a pet sheep and riding a pig, just because Dad said I could, still make me smile.

Looking back through my now-adult eyes, I see things so differently and hopefully more clearly. I see my father as a young man full of energy and hope for the future, trying his best to succeed and provide for his family. I can vividly recall the look of concern and lack of sleep that came when the ground was too dry or when it rained too much while he waited for the crops to produce. The weight he bore was much heavier than a child needed to realize. And because he loved me, he did his best to protect me from those burdens. Seeds of doubt and discouragement were often loads that daddy carried. So-called 'loved ones' were quick to water and fertilize these seeds in his young heart. No one knew of the hurt he bore except for my momma and his Lord. Our Lord always knows!

Pondering these feelings of inadequacy and fear, one day he fell upon a simple Scripture verse that changed the course of his life forever. "But seek ye FIRST the kingdom of God and His righteousness, and all these things shall be added to you." Matthew 6:33 (NKJV). Speaking to his young heart, God said, "You put me first, and I'll take care of you!" And may I add, He continues to do so!

Dear reader, this simple truth is a promise to everyone who is in Christ! Whether we live our lives on a public platform or a day-to-day nine-to-five job, God says, "Put me first, and I'll take care of you!"

Please hear my heart — this is not a health/wealth gospel! Trials come, and life will hurt. (John 16:33) But oh, what a ride it can be if we keep our eyes on the Savior! It reminds me of the time that Dad put me on that pig. It started to run, and I was scared! But my father was right there, running alongside, waiting to catch me if I fell. Our Heavenly Father does the same.

Clay Huff Christmas

Excitement filled the air that evening in our little Elementary School. It was the annual PTA Christmas program, and Mrs. Kennedy's third-grade class was ready to take the stage! I don't remember the title of our little production, but I certainly remember the theme! Like the classic TV Christmas special, we were the leftover toys no one wanted. Tommy was a firefighter with his own truck, Liz played a jack-in-the-box, and I was a ballerina!

We were each given solos to sing, and I was so impressed by Liz and Tommy's vocal abilities that I just knew they were going to be famous someday! I still remember the song I sang that night. Its words were simple, but the message was so strong that it still causes me to pause even today.

*"I wonder what Christmas is like,
When you're not left on the shelf...
I wonder what Christmas is like,
When you're not left over like me."*

The message is nothing new. If we would only take a moment to look, we would see them everywhere. The empty, broken, and lonely are closer than we think, wishing and hoping that someone, somewhere, would reach out and care.

In Matthew 22:37-39 (NKJV), Jesus said, "You shall love the LORD your God with all your heart, with all your soul, and with all your mind. This is the first and greatest commandment, and the second is like it: You shall love your neighbor as yourself."

We've become so accustomed to giving a few extra dollars to help those less fortunate, and that's good! But I don't believe that's what Jesus meant when He called us to love God and then others. Loving as God has commanded isn't always easy. It requires sacrifice. Giving of our time, lending a listening ear, or just being available can be a challenge! But oh, the reward of being able to share Jesus, however we can! Yes, giving a little money and walking away would be easier. However, I'm reminded that Jesus did just the opposite for me. He came to this evil world and gave everything He had to purchase me so I would no longer be left on that shelf. He proved His own love for me by dying while I was yet a sinner. (Romans 5:8) He did the same for you.

Matthew 25: 35-36, 40b (NKJV), "For I was hungry and you gave me food. I was thirsty, and you gave Me a drink. I was a stranger and you took Me in. I was naked and you clothed Me. I was sick and you visited Me. I was in prison and you came to Me. Assuredly, I say to you, inasmuch as you did it to one of the least of these, My brethren, You did it to Me."

Dear reader, life is short. Let's reach out and love.

Crying Out to God

"...the Father of mercies and the God of all comfort..."
-2 Corinthians 1:3b

Have you ever tried crying out to the Lord, but the words just wouldn't come? There have been times I've been so broken that all I could do was fall on my knees and weep. But because God is my Father, I know He heard me. If you're His child, He hears your cries, too. If that's where you are today, may I offer some reassurance? Paul tells us in Romans 8:26-27 (NKJV), "the Spirit also helps in our weakness. For we do not know what we should pray for as we ought, but the Spirit Himself makes intercession for us with groanings which cannot be uttered. Now He who searches the heart knows what the mind of the Spirit is because He makes intercession for the saints according to the will of God."

God may seem silent right now, but I can assure you that if you're His child, He sees, He hears, He cares, and He's working all things together for your good. Don't give in to the lies the enemy is throwing your way. God is STILL in control! Even though you may not understand now, one day it will all make sense...one day. God cannot lie (Numbers 23:19, Titus 1:2), and He promises never to leave or forsake you. (Deuteronomy 31:6,8, Hebrews 13:5)

I love how David was reassured by the Lord when he penned the words in Psalm 34:15, 17-18 (NKJV): "The eyes of the LORD are on the righteous, and His ears are open to their cry for help. The righteous cry out, and the LORD hears and rescues them from all their troubles. The LORD is near the brokenhearted; He saves those crushed in spirit."

Never forget, dear reader, God loves you more than any man, woman, or child ever could. He proved it when He sent His son to die in your place. He's got it all under control.

Encouragement

Recently, a woman I didn't know approached me while out and about. After introducing herself, she simply wanted to share how a devotional I had written ministered to her. She didn't share the details but just wanted to encourage me in the ministry. Little did she know how much I needed that word on that day. I'm so thankful that she listened to the prompting of the Holy Spirit and spoke to me.

In Romans 1, as Paul was writing to help lay the foundation of the church, he first encouraged them in their work." First, I thank my God through Jesus Christ for all of you because the news of your faith is being reported worldwide!" Can you just imagine the encouragement they felt as they read those words? He then goes on to say, "For I long to see you, that I may impart to you some spiritual gift, so that you may be established - that is, that I may be encouraged together with you by the mutual faith both of you and me." Throughout Scripture, we can see how God used His people to encourage others. And He wants to use YOU to do the same. A kind word like I received, a smile, a card, a phone call, or perhaps a bit more of your time is all it will take to encourage another soul. Will you step out and be the one?

Flip Phone Hubby

Recently, my husband, who still insists on using a flip phone, discovered a whole new world of listening pleasure through the use of my 'more sophisticated' smartphone. He had no idea there was an entire realm of music, sermons, books, and podcasts we could enjoy anytime, anywhere!

Next to listening to wonderful messages from some of today's solid Bible teachers and preachers, he enjoys documentaries on the mafia and other true crime stories. Quite a contrast, I must admit.

One weekend, my sweet, mild-mannered flip phone guy and I traveled to West Virginia for two scheduled engagements. Our destination was about a seven-hour drive from home, and I was looking forward to getting away and doing what I had been called to do.

Before hitting the road, my guy indicated that he was looking forward to listening to a True Crime podcast we had recently discovered. Truth be known, I was, too! Some of the stories told can keep you on the edge of your seat with anticipation, waiting for the next move with bated breath! And so, with the car loaded, our destination clear, seatbelts on, and coffee in hand, that's *exactly* what we did! All the way there and back!

Actual events full of mystery, intrigue, twists, turns, lies, and murder filled the air! Real people with genuine souls, living their lives away from Christ, with destruction as their end! There was no sign of falling asleep at the wheel on this journey!

By the time we had returned home, I pointed out the fact that throughout the weekend, we had listened to almost fifteen hours of violence, deception, murder, oppression, hopelessness, and fear! I almost felt like I needed to get in the house, lock the doors, and wait until Jesus came to take me home! I truly felt a weight on my shoulders!

However, the Holy Spirit quickly broke through those dark thoughts with the light of God's word and reminded me of what we had just heard that morning from our host Pastor. Nahum 1:7 (NKJV) says, "The LORD is good, a stronghold in the day of trouble; And He knows those who trust in Him."

Yes, dear reader, this world is full of despair, trouble, and fear. At this very moment, you may be able to see it and its effects as you look into the mirror of your own life! But, for the Born-Again-Believer, we know that Jesus is our stronghold!

I'm comforted that the One who flung the stars into space and gave them each a name is my Father! I don't have to fear because my Heavenly Daddy promises He'll never leave or forsake me. I trust Him.

This is true for every child of God! Fear should never take over our lives! Yes, we must be cautious and keep a constant lookout. The Word tells us to do that very thing in Ephesians 6:10-18, but *never* in fear! He *is* your stronghold. You can trust Him to see you through.

Answered Prayer Through a Simple Song

    This morning, I reflected on letters and prayers I've written to the Lord. Some, I will never share with anyone. The gut-wrenching cries that have flowed from my heart to the Throne are for my Savior alone, for He's the only one who truly understands. He listens without judgment. No one can hear or touch me like He does.

    We all cry out to the Lord for many reasons: forgiveness, His touch, His reassurance, a blessing, an open door, or other needs. However, when the answer comes, we often forget to praise and thank Him!

    But today, dear reader, for just a moment, peek into my window. Because the Lord is leading me to do so, I want you to hear, in part, one of those prayers and then the answer to show you how wonderful my Jesus is.

~~~~~

Sept 4, 2019

    "Help me, Lord! I'm drowning in myself to the point that I feel as if I'm dying spiritually! My song falls flat even to my own ears! I read your Word every day, searching, and yet I'm still numb."

    "Sing to me, Lord, and melt my heart. Draw me to Yourself and hold me! Look into my eyes and tell me again that You love me. Search me, I beg of you! Show me my sin, and I will repent! Then, forgive me. Hug me so tight that I'll never forget Your touch as I sing and speak to others about Your mercy, grace, and everlasting love from which nothing can separate us...." As I re-read this plea, the Holy Spirit reminded me of something else I had written a few weeks AFTER I had cried out.

~~~~~~~~

Oct 9, 2019

I'm an early riser. The Lord will usually wake me around 4:00 a.m. to spend time together before the world and its distractions start crashing in. Many mornings, without being conscious of it, I awake with a song playing somewhere in the background of my mind. It's not one of those annoying times when you can't get a song out of your head. This is different. It's like the song is being sung TO me.

This morning, I awoke to yet another one. It wasn't blaring; it was a soft, soothing whisper that seemed to gradually envelop me. Imagine, if you will, Christmas Carolers singing in the distance. You can hear the music but can't quite make out the tune until they get closer. The closer they get, the louder they become. When they reach your place, you hear the melody ringing loud and clear, and you can't help but sing along!

Most mornings, before the covers are off and my feet hit the floor, I usually tell the Lord good morning and pray. Today, however, I heard the song almost immediately. Still, it was so soft I didn't pay much attention to it. It's hard to explain, but it was there. As I made my way into the next room, there was a quick crescendo! Suddenly, its beautiful words filled my soul, and I quickly realized that the Lord was singing to me, reminding me...

"Jesus loves me, this I know,
For the Bible tells me so;
Little ones to Him belong,
They are weak, but He is strong.
Yes, Jesus loves me,
Yes, Jesus loves me,
Yes, Jesus loves me;
The Bible tells me so!"

When I realized what was happening, I dropped my head, smiled, and said, "Lord, I love you too. Thank you for that." I was overwhelmed by His presence! The Holy Spirit was singing and speaking to me! Zeph. 3:17 (NKJV) says, "The Lord your God is in your midst, The Mighty One will save; He will rejoice over you with gladness, He will quiet you with His love, He will rejoice over you with singing." There's a song that says, "He still speaks, I know his voice." John 10:27 (CSB) says, "My sheep hear my voice, I know them, and they follow me." It's personal. It's joyous. And, it's sacred.

Therefore, as long as He allows me and I have breath to do so, "I will sing to the Lord as long as I live; I will sing praise to my God while I have my being. May the meditation be sweet to Him; I will be glad in the Lord." - Psalm 104:33-34 (NKJV) I pray this for you as well, dear reader. He's right there, right where you are at this very moment. He has heard your cries. Listen! Can you hear Him?

My Greatest Love

No matter how old I get, I'll never forget that Thursday evening in June 1970. That night, right before my tenth birthday, I was forever changed, and the greatest love story of my life began to unfold. No, I didn't meet my future (earthly) husband. I was, how-ever, introduced to the One who loved me perfectly. Quickly, He wrapped me in His arms, washed my dirty heart clean, and made me His own.

Up to this point in my young life, I had only heard stories in Sunday school about this One, but it wasn't until that night that we met face to face. He was the One who promised He would never leave or forsake me. Jesus — the Lover of my soul. Today, I'm called His bride. How can I describe a love so great? Mere words flowing from my mouth or through a writer's pen will always fall short. Try as I may, I can't wrap my mind around the fact that God, the creator of the universe, so loved me that He sent his only Son to die so I could live! He said all I needed to do was believe in Him, and we would be together forever! (John 3:16)

Throughout the ensuing years, the Lord has proven time and again just how faithful and perfect His love is. I could share many stories of how He's helped me climb mountains and held me close in the valleys. I could also tell you of the times I've stood and praised Him for all He has done in my life, for He alone is worthy. However, I could also share with you that my love for my Savior has often fallen short.

More times than I'd like to admit, I've taken the

glory that belongs to Him alone for myself. I've even turned my back and done things my way, failing miserably. Yet, because His love is perfect, when I come to Him in repentance, I find grace, mercy, and forgiveness (1 John 1:9). Oh, how He loves me!

The good news is that this love story is not just for me; it's for anyone who desires a love that never fails! Jesus, the One who gave His life, desires a relationship with you! "For God so loved the WORLD that He gave His only begotten Son, that WHOEVER believes in Him should not perish but have everlasting life!" John 3:13 (NKJV)

"Love consists in this: not that we loved God, but that He loved us and sent His Son to be the atoning sacrifice for our sins." (1 John 4:10 CSB)

"But God demonstrates His own love toward us, in that while we were still sinners, Christ died for us." (Romans 5:8 NKJV)

Dear reader, if you've never met Jesus face to face and desire a personal relationship with the One who loves you more than anyone ever could, send me a message. I would love the opportunity to go through scripture and pray with you. He's worth it!

Friendship

"...but I have called you friends..." - John 15:15

Navigating those awkward teenage years can undoubtedly be a challenge. I know I had mine, especially regarding friendships. Don't get me wrong; I had plenty of friends! There were nights when our house was full of laughter and giggles. Memories of sleeping bags and pillows scattered everywhere, while Mom served up homemade pizza from a box, still make me smile. One of those friends still shares that our house was the first place she ever had leftover pizza for breakfast!

But even with all those friends, I still felt a loneliness I could never shake. Often feeling like a "fifth wheel," I constantly desired that "one friend" with whom I could share all my secrets while she shared hers. Proverbs 18:24 (NKJV) says, "A man who has friends must himself be friendly, but there is a friend who sticks closer than a brother." I found that Friend — His name is Jesus! Yes, He is the King of kings, the Lord of lords, and the Master of everything! He is the Creator and Sustainer. There is none like Him — He is God! Yet, He's also the best friend I've ever had. For you see:

He loves me — John 3:16
He listens to me — Psalm 5:3
He's honest with me — Titus 1:2
He gave His life for me — John 15:13
He will always be by my side — Deuteronomy 31:6, Hebrews 13:5

He's preparing a place just for me, so that I can live with Him forever — John 14:3

As time passes, I realize just how fortunate I am. My life is filled with close friends! The Lord has placed so many along my path who have listened to my heart and prayed for me as I shared my joys and sorrows. Each friendship is unique in its own way, and I cherish them all! Many have also confided deep secrets, longings, disappointments, trials, and triumphs with me that will never be told to another soul. I hold them all close and am honored that they felt comfortable enough to share them with me. Yet I wonder — could it be that the Lord placed that void in my soul for a special friend to prove to me that He alone is the only One who could fill it? I believe so.

Mirror, Mirror

"We are ambassadors for Christ, as though God were pleading through us..." - 2 Corinthians 5:20

"Mirror, mirror on the wall, I've become my mother, after all!" Knowing that I resemble her is an honor—she's a beautiful woman, both inside and out! Honestly, I don't even have to look in the mirror to see the resemblance. All I need to do is examine my hands, feet, and knees while standing next to her to know that I am truly her offspring. More than once, I have sensed her reflection within me, simply by the way I was standing! Recently, I heard my father chuckle as he remarked on how much I look like her. From my perspective, watching her provides a small glimpse into my future, if the Lord allows. If I could be half the wife, mother, grandmother, and, most importantly, the woman of God that she is, I'd be thrilled!

While I'm honored to resemble my sweet momma, there's One whose image I long to reflect even more—my precious Jesus. It's easy to connect me with my mother—our looks and mannerisms give it all away! But what about the life I lead on a daily basis? Do my actions and my mannerisms reflect the One who loves me best and loves me most?

I love how Luke describes an incident in Acts 4:13 (NKJV): "Now when they saw the boldness of Peter and John, and perceived that they were uneducated and untrained men, they marveled. And they realized that they had been with Jesus". They reflected the image of the

Father!

When people look at me, can they see that I, too, have been with Jesus? Can they tell by simply observing me who my Father is? Does my walk align with my talk? Does the kindness I strive to show reflect the love of Christ, regardless of the circumstance? Does the light of Christ shine through me to the point that when people see my good works, they will glorify only my Father in Heaven? (Matthew 5:16) Do others desire a relationship with my Father because of what they see in me? "Oh Lord, shine through me!"

Dear reader, as I claim the name of Christ, these are difficult questions I need to ask myself every day! So should you. I've said many times, "I don't always get it right," but I'm thankful for my heavenly Daddy who loves me enough to correct me when I fail and gives me the opportunity to try again.

I hope that one day I can change my little banter to the following: "Mirror, mirror on the wall, I'm looking like Jesus after all!"

But we all, with unveiled faces, beholding as in a mirror the glory of the Lord, are being transformed into the same image from glory to glory, just as by the Spirit of the Lord. (2 Cor. 3:18)

Open Bible

When I was a child living at home, I remember feeling very afraid one night. I don't know why I didn't go and wake my parents, as they were never the type to get angry if disturbed. Instead, I did something I had never done before. I took my Bible, opened it, and placed it on my dresser. In my childlike mind, I trusted that open Book to keep me safe by warding off whatever caused my fear!

Can I share a little secret? There are nights when I still sleep with my Bible open. Most recently, my husband had to be out of town, and I was home alone. On the pillow where his head would have rested next to mine, the Word lay open to Psalm 56:3 (NKJV), which says, "When I am afraid, I will trust in You." I slept well that night.

A few months ago, uneasiness had crept into my soul while traveling by myself. As I began to pray for the Lord's peace and protection, I once again pulled out God's Word and laid it open on the car seat beside me. This time, the words from 2 Timothy 1:7 (NKJV) served as a visible reminder of His presence: "For God has not given us a spirit of fear, but of power and of love and a sound mind."

The Author of this book also happens to be my best friend. He calls me His child and wrote this love letter to me even before I was! In fact, He tells me in Proverbs 18:24b that He's a friend who sticks closer than a brother! In Hebrews 13:5, He promises never to leave or forsake me! He even went so far as to prove just how much He loves me by sending Jesus, His only Son, to DIE for my sins! (John 3:16) He concludes this letter by reassuring me that one day, He'll return to take me and my brothers and sisters to His home to live for eternity! He calls us His Bride.

Yes, I hold my Bible close. The Holy Spirit uses it to breathe assurance and guidance into my soul every day. I don't fully understand it all, but I believe the words written on its pages are true.

So today, I think I'll place it open to Ephesians 3:22-23 as a reminder: "Now to Him who is able to do exceedingly abundantly above all that I could ever ask or think, according to the power that works in us, to Him be glory in the church by Christ Jesus throughout the ages, world without end. Amen!" Ephesians 3:20-21 (NKJV)

Piano Recital

When I was a little girl, my piano teacher had me sing a song for the annual recital she hosted. I felt nervous and scared, but I'll never forget the words from my young lips.

"Let there be peace on earth, and let it begin with me..."

Hatred, war, and death are pervasive, and they will persist until the Lord's return. However, it appears to have escalated even more this year in our homeland. An unseen virus and politics have divided families and friends like I have never experienced in my lifetime. Sadly, some of this horrible unrest has made its way into our Christian homes.

Dear reader, please hear my heart! As Born-Again Children of God, we must NEVER back down, lay down, or compromise the truth of God's word. We MUST stand firm in and on it! Why? Because people are watching US! And WHY are they watching? As believers, we claim to possess the true peace they're seeking, and they want to see if it's real!

Jesus said in John 14:27 (NAS) "Peace, I leave with you; My peace I give to you; Not as the world gives do I give to you. Do not let your heart be troubled, nor let it be fearful." Then in Romans 12:18 (NKJV) we find, "If possible, as much as depends on you,
Live peaceably with all men."

Ponder this with me: If those of us who claim the name of Jesus would practice what we preached by living out that peace, could it be that God would use us to point those who have no peace to the TRUE Prince of Peace? I believe the answer is yes!

Peace - what a wonderful gift to give this year! *"Let there be peace on earth, And let it begin with me!"*

"Let There Be Peace on Earth" -
Written by Jill Jackson-Miller and Sy Miller, 1955

Restoration

"But those who wait on the Lord shall renew their strength..."
- Isaiah 40:31

Today, the Holy Spirit reminded me that this is not merely a "promise given" but a "Promise fulfilled."

Our little church has seen its share of heartache. We began to reach our lowest point just a few years ago when, one by one, folks were quietly slipping out to seek other places for worship. There was no quarreling, but something was missing in our Body and they needed to find it. To be honest, my husband and I also thought about leaving, but the Lord would never release us. Not wanting to be out of His will, we stayed. With barely enough people to keep the doors open, we then found ourselves without a pastor. God had indeed stripped us down to the bare remnant.

As we waited for the Lord to move, our prayer for guidance and unity was strong and consistent. As a result, our hearts began to knit together in a way we had never known before. We were different! And that's when God began to rebuild us. A year and a half later, God sent His man.

Today, the Holy Spirit is on the move, and people are being saved! Our tired souls have been renewed with a love for each other and the lost like we've never known!

This takes me back to Isaiah 40:31.. "But those who wait upon the Lord shall renew their strength, they shall mount up with wings as eagles, they shall run and not grow weary, they shall walk and not faint..."

    Oh, dear reader, this isn't just a promise given to our little flock, it's for every child of God! Keep praying and keep holding on to the only ONE who can see you through, and one day, you, too, will see the promise fulfilled.

Seneca Rock

Doughnuts! Who doesn't love one or two of these sweet treats alongside a good cup of coffee to start the day? I smile as I recall when the Lord taught me a thing or two about how a doughnut can relate to my walk with Him.

Many years ago, when our son Philip was around ten years old, we embarked on a trip to the beautiful state of West Virginia. Before setting out on our adventure, my husband Greg mentioned that he wanted to stop and visit a state park called Seneca Rock. That night, we arrived in a quaint little town nestled in the mountains, where we found lodging. When morning arrived, my boys enjoyed a nutritious breakfast while I chose a doughnut. This proved to be a bad idea because I had no clue of what we were about to do!

Around mid-morning, we arrived at the park and toured the visitor center. A massive window inside the building allowed visitors to look out and see the main attraction—a large rock at the top of the mountain. Greg exclaimed, "Let's climb it!" With my mouth hanging open, I looked at him and said, "All I had for breakfast was a doughnut, and you expect me to climb that mountain?" Philip, of course, thought it would be fun, so I tried not to be a "Debbie Downer" and agreed. Honestly, I didn't want to ruin the day by expressing my thoughts, but the Lord heard them anyway. As we walked, I whispered, "Lord, this is not going to work!"

About halfway up the mountain, I began to feel weak and shaky as this somewhat enjoyable adventure quickly did a nose-dive. I could go no further and said, "Boys, I'm done! The doughnut's gone, and I'm going to sit right here and wait until you come back." Of course, they were disappointed and tried to encourage me to press on, but at this point, I simply couldn't. I assured them that I would be right there, awaiting their return.

Sitting there alone, I watched other climbers press forward, ascending the steep incline. I also listened to the joyful chatter from those who were returning from the top, basking in what they had seen and experienced.

As I regained some strength, I climbed up to the next small plateau. From there, I could see the top of the massive rock and its impressive presence jutting out of the mountain; a glorious sight to behold. It was then I heard the sweet voice of the Holy Spirit whisper to my heart, "Greg and Philip are going to make it to the top of this mountain! When they do, they'll look out over My creation and be in awe of what they see! But because you didn't have the proper nutrition and gave up before you made it to the top, all you'll experience is what THEY tell you."

"This is how so many of my children live their lives," He continued. "They fill themselves with 'spiritual doughnuts,' never taking in the proper nutrition from Me or my Word, feasting instead on the world's empty delicacies. They're convinced that filling a pew and hearing a sermon once a week is enough. Walking in their own strength, they make it for a while, but when they face life's mountains, they don't get very far. In a weakened spiritual state, they simply sit down and quit, often blaming Me for their problems."

"Moreover," He said, "as they stay on the sidelines, they begin to watch in awe as others endure the climb, making it to the top. With no testimony of their own because of poor choices, all they hear and see is the joy from someone else's journey." I hung my head in shame.

The Apostle Paul sat in prison facing a huge mountain when he said, "… but one thing I do, forgetting those things which are behind and reaching forward to those things which are ahead, I press toward the goal for the prize of the upward call of God in Christ Jesus." Phil 3: 13b-14 (NKJV). Then several verses later, he said, "I can do all things through Christ who strengthens me." Phil 4:13 (NKJV). Paul knew full well the need for continuous spiritual nourishment.

Oh dear reader, the Lord does not desire for you to live your life undernourished and on the sidelines with no testimony of your own to share. We all have mountains to face in this life. But, it's only when we are feeding daily on the Lord and His Word that we can rest assured He walks beside us, providing the strength we need to climb.

Testimony Time

Testimony time! Remember those special moments during worship service? You could always count on one or two faithful souls to stand and give praise to the Lord for His goodness. Most were quick and to the point, followed by a chorus of "Hallelujahs!" and "Amens!"

From time to time, there'd be that "one" who would weave a tale of sin and shame, confessing everything all over again to the entire congregation. I vividly remember one such evening when the pastor had to cut in before everyone was embarrassed!

A few years ago, I was scheduled to sing in a church not far from my home. Just before I was to begin, the pastor asked if anyone had a testimony they'd like to share. A young man stood and spoke of his sinful past and how God had gloriously saved him! When he finished, everyone said, "Amen!" Excitedly, the pastor looked at a lady sitting not far from me and asked her to speak. That's when my heart broke.

Slowly standing with her head hung low, this sweet lady began. "I really don't have a testimony," she said. "I've never been addicted to drugs or alcohol, and I've never been arrested! I know I'm saved, but I have nothing exciting to share!" Sadly, to my own shame, I left that evening without pouring any encouragement into her downtrodden soul.

Oh, dear reader, let's focus on the fact that Jesus DIED so that you and I could LIVE! That's our testimony! Whether your life was a tangled mess or you came to

Christ as a child sitting in Sunday school, give him PRAISE for all He has done! He snatched you from eternal death and gave you eternal life! Oh, what a Savior! I strongly encourage you to read the entire chapter of Psalm 103; for now, consider these verses.

2. Bless the LORD, O my soul, and forget not all of His benefits:

3. Who forgives all your iniquities, Who heals all your diseases,

4. Who redeems your life from destruction...

8. The LORD is merciful and gracious, slow to anger, and abounding in mercy....

10. He has not dealt with us according to our sins, nor punished us according to our iniquities...

Now, THAT'S a testimony worthy of praise!

The Man on the Street

I only saw him briefly as we drove past, but it's an image the Lord has emblazoned on my heart and mind forever. Sitting on the grass with his back to the traffic, I noticed that his feet were bare and his clothes were torn and tattered. Although I could only see him from behind, his bent body still could not conceal the shame he tried to hide. The man was broken and homeless.

This familiar scene shows no respect for people. Men, women, and children - people created in the image of God - are living on the streets, begging and/or selling themselves for food, money, drugs, or alcohol, doing anything to survive while crying out for love and care. Yes, some find themselves in this position due to lifestyle choices, but many genuinely have no place to go and no one to turn to. Either way, they remain empty and broken.

As I ponder the scene from that day, I see that it's no longer just the homeless man. While his physical needs were very real, it was as if, through this one man, I could perceive the souls of all humanity without Christ. The rich, the poor, and those in between are torn, tattered, empty, and alone. I see people hungry for true peace, love, and hope, crying out for someone to care.

Our outward appearance will never tell the complete story. The lovely home, fancy car, beautiful face, and stylish clothes can never reveal what's inside a man's soul. Yet, so often, that's how we judge one's worth.

The Word is clear in Eph 2:11-12: "Without Christ, we have no hope, no place to call home." Without Christ, you and I are poor in spirit, without hope for the riches of knowing Him. Without Christ, our hearts and lives are broken by the world's promises that will never satisfy. Without Christ, we will *always* be captive to the sin of this world and our fleshly desires.

But there IS hope! Jesus said in Luke 4: 18-20 (KJV), "The Spirit of the Lord is upon Me because He hath anointed me to preach the Gospel to the poor; He hath sent me to heal the broken-hearted, to preach deliverance to the captives, and recovering of sight to the blind, to set at liberty them that are bruised."

Without Christ, we will always be battered, bruised, blind, hopeless, with no place to call home. But, *with* Christ? There's freedom, healing, forgiveness, and hope! The door is open…come home. He's calling your name.

Watchful Eye

Growing up, I could never get away with anything! Being an only child until I was fifteen, there was no one else in the house on whom I could cast the blame! In addition to this, "a great cloud of witnesses" had constant access to my parents...my grade-school teachers!

As far as I was concerned, there was never a need to schedule a parent-teacher conference. Mom had a private audience with each teacher at least four times a month, whether needed or not. As their hairdresser, each of those precious ladies, kindergarten through 5th grade, had a standing, weekly appointment with her! When I finally reached the 6th grade, I thought I had found a reprieve since my teacher was now a man, but that dream was short-lived — he was married to my 4th-grade teacher!

Through all of this, I was also well aware that if I got into trouble at school, an even stiffer punishment awaited at home. However, this is not the appropriate time to speak about the spanking I received that afternoon when Mrs. P. showed up right on time for her weekly hairdo!

Riding the school bus was no different. When I was in the 4th grade, Dad landed his first bus route as a driver, and of course, it was my job to set the example as a well-behaved child for everyone else. Until I reached high school, he was my daily escort. The baton was then handed off to the next driver who passed by our house — my grandfather. I was covered on every side! Looking back, I was blessed without even realizing it!

As a Born-Again Child of God, there are days I fail

to remember just how blessed and covered I am by His hand. I'm sure more than a few things slipped past my parents' ever-watchful eye, but my God sees and hears it all.

Psalm 139: 2-6 (NKJV)
"2 You know my sitting down and my rising up; You understand my thoughts afar off, 3 You comprehend my path and my lying down, and are acquainted with all my ways. 4 For there is not a word on my tongue but behold, O Lord, You know it altogether 5 You have hedged me behind and before and laid Your hand upon me. 6 Such knowledge is too wonderful for me. It is high; I cannot attain it."

God sees and hears all that we say and do, taking action on our behalf. Because He loves us so much, sometimes that action includes the blessing of discipline. I'll never forget the spanking I received from my daddy on that day so many years ago. I know he loved me, yet I had broken his heart and needed to understand what I had done was wrong. The punishment I received was deserved.

Proverbs 3:11-12 (CSB) says, "Do not despise the LORD'S instruction, my son, and do not loathe his discipline, for the LORD disciplines the one he loves, just as a father disciplines the son in whom he delights."

Recently, my Heavenly Father saw fit to raise His hand of discipline again for me. I had broken His heart, and He needed to let me know. I must admit it hurt, and I cried. But, because He loves me, it was necessary. I'm thankful, and I am blessed!

So today, dear reader, let's take the time to thank the Lord for His constant watch over us and the times of discipline, even when it hurts. Then, realize how blessed you are. Why? Because you are loved!

Where is Peace

I broke down this week. I took my eyes off the Lord and started looking at the mess around me. I allowed the political chaos, civil unrest, and a worldwide pandemic to consume me with fear and sadness. Like you, I've heard of areas where large, violent protests are considered appropriate while church gatherings are deemed dangerous. The possibility of more shutdowns threatens the livelihood and sanity of some of my closest loved ones. Also, like you, I've been mandated to wear a mask and socially distance myself in order to protect myself and others from getting sick. Depression and suicide are on the rise for those already alone due to the lack of human touch and interaction. Yes, I broke, and it wasn't pretty.

However, in my distress, the Holy Spirit broke through and reminded me that God was not surprised by any of this and that He was still in control. I was then reminded of a scripture that David wrote while he, too, was in turmoil. Psalm 42:11 (CSB) says, "Why, my soul, are you so dejected? Why are you in such turmoil? Put your hope in God, for I will still praise Him, my Savior and my God." I then went to Philippians, where Paul encouraged Believers to give thanks with joy!

So often, we fail to remember that this innocent man wrote the following words from a prison cell! Chapter 4:4-9 (CSB) says, "Rejoice in the Lord always! I will say it again: Rejoice! Let your graciousness be known to everyone. The Lord is near. Don't worry about anything, but in everything, through prayer and thanksgiving, present your requests to God. And the peace of

God, which surpasses all understanding, will guard your hearts and minds in Christ Jesus. Finally, brothers and sisters, whatever is true, whatever is honorable, whatever is just, whatever is pure, whatever is lovely, whatever is commendable - if there is any moral excellence and if there is anything praiseworthy - dwell on these things. Do what you have learned, received, heard, and seen in me, and the God of peace will be with you."

So, dear reader, do not despair as I did. Whatever your situation, never forget that the God we serve is bigger and stronger than anything the enemy can throw our way. Let's keep our eyes on the prize!

Angels Unaware

"For I was hungry and you gave me something to eat."
- Matthew 25:35

Having different guests around the dinner table was common in my childhood home. Traveling Evangelists, large family get-togethers, our Pastor's family, missionaries, and friends all seemed to find their way to our house. Evidence has been shown many times that my parents were indeed given the spiritual gift of hospitality! It seems as if they never met a stranger!

Just a few years ago, however, my father took this special gift a bit further than anyone might have imagined.

Late one evening, my mother called asking how many eggs I had to spare. She needed bread and any other breakfast items that I could get to her. When I learned that Dad was headed home with a family of seven (three generations) who had been stranded along the interstate, I packed up what she needed and quickly got it to her. At that time, we lived in a rural area with no motels nearby, which meant there was no place to stay. Additionally, the local garage was closed for the night. This family of strangers was completely stranded. Time and space do not afford me to tell you how Dad came across these folks in the first place, but I believe it was just a God moment.

Early the next morning, Mom was already working in the beauty salon she operated out of their home, before the guests awoke. However, before her first customer arrived, she set the table and prepared a meal fit for a king. After Dad shared breakfast with the travelers, he returned them to their car, which his mechanic was already repairing. Once the thank-you's and goodbyes were exchanged, the strangers went on their way, never to be heard of again.

Hebrews 13:1-2 (CSB) says, "Let brotherly love continue. Don't neglect to show hospitality, for by doing this, some have welcomed angels as guests without knowing it."

Over the years, we have often pondered that moment in time, wondering — did we entertain some of the angels that Hebrews speaks of, or was this a very real family in desperate need? At this point, only the Lord knows, and that's OK!

However, that one instance reminds me to be constantly alert. God may bring one soul across my path today that needs His divine intervention. My prayer is that I will be sensitive to His leading to use the gifts He has given me, to be the hands and feet to carry out His will. Either way, Matthew 25:35-36, 40b (CSB) sums it up perfectly. "For I was hungry and you gave me something to eat; I was thirsty and you gave me something to drink; I was a stranger and you took my in; I was naked and you clothed me; I was sick and you took care of me; I was in prison and you visited me. "Truly I tell you, whatever you did for one of the least of these brothers and sisters of mine, you did for me."

Broken Pastor

I had just finished setting up my sound equipment for the concert when he walked into the church that Sunday morning. Without saying a word, I could see sadness in his eyes that broke my heart.

He smiled and greeted me with a pleasant tenderness, but the unspoken burden he carried overshadowed his kindness. Although I didn't know the man well, one thing was certain—he was broken. He was also the pastor.

After greeting the crowd and asking the Lord's blessing on the service, this man of God quickly turned the next hour over to me. I prayed without ceasing as I sang, read Scripture, and testified. This had nothing to do with me, but I asked the Lord to use me to encourage this man who was grieving! During the altar time, he was the first to come and fall on his knees before his Lord. What I witnessed next broke my heart—not one person came to pray with or encourage him! Not one!

His congregation dearly loved this pastor. From the moment I arrived at the church, until I left, his people had nothing but praise for this dear man! So why did they not rally around him to pray in his hour of grief?

1 Thessalonians 5:11a says, "Comfort each other", while Galatians 6:2 instructs to, "Bear one another's burdens and fulfill the law of Christ."

I'm not judging them, but just trying to understand. Could it be they didn't know how? Perhaps they feared overstepping their bounds because he was "The Pastor?"

Many years ago, when I began my journey in Women's Ministry, I came face-to-face with the fact that the loneliest woman in the church is often the pastor's wife. Pressing in further, I then learned an even more complicated truth: the pastor's entire family is usually the loneliest one within the congregation!

Dear church member, this ought not to be so! I don't believe excluding these precious souls is something we intentionally set out to do, but we, including myself, have done it nonetheless.

Speaking with my pastor about a horrific time in his ministry years earlier, I asked him, "Whom did you have to lean on during that time?" His response was, "I had no one. People would ask about the situation or others involved, but no one ever asked how I was doing, and it hurt. I was alone."

Many years ago, I remember our former pastor reading the following scripture. But before he read it, he said, "This is what I ask of you." "Continue earnestly in prayer, being vigilant in it with thanksgiving; MEANWHILE praying also for [me] that God would open to [me] a door for the Word, to speak the mystery of Christ, for which I am also in chains, that I may make manifest, as I ought to speak." - Colossians 4:2-4 (NKJV) In other words, he was asking us to please pray for him!

There is a particular honor and respect for privacy that we must hold onto when it comes to our pastors. These anointed men of God have been called to a serious task to shepherd the flock of Christ, and one day they will stand before the Lord and give an account. (Hebrews 13:17) Besides teaching and leading us, they also have a precious family to love and provide for. I can only imagine the heaviness of the weight they carry.

But never forget, dear reader, at the end of the day, they are flesh and blood in need of friendship, encouragement, and prayer. And one day, you and I will also give an account of how we took care of them. "And we urge you, brethren, to recognize those who labor among you, and to esteem them very highly in love, for their work's sake."- 1 Thessalonians 5:12-13a (NKJV)

Decaf Please

It had been a long weekend, and all I wanted was a cup of decaf coffee to keep me company as I drove home. Once I spotted those familiar Golden Arches, I knew my taste buds would soon be satisfied. The young lady behind the counter, however, was having a bad day and did not share my enthusiasm for the sacred bean.

Before placing my order, I kindly asked, "Is the decaf fresh?" She gave a half shrug as if she didn't know and didn't care! Flashing my best Jesus smile, I said, "Would it be possible to please make a fresh pot?" With some smart aleck grunt, she said, "Well, it'll take me a few minutes!" My smile quickly faded right along with my Christ-like attitude, which in turn allowed my flesh to rise to the occasion! "Never mind, then!" as I quickly turned and walked out the door.

I didn't get very far down the road before the Holy Spirit began to speak. His voice wasn't audible, mind you, but I heard Him nonetheless. "Why did you act that way?" He said. You just spoke to a group of ladies about the importance of representing Me no matter where they are, and then you speak to someone you don't even know, with total disrespect! You have no clue as to what that young lady is facing today!" Conviction flooded my soul, and I began to repent. However, the Lord wasn't finished, and the conversation continued.

"I want you to turn this car around and go back and apologize to her". "But, Lord!" I argued! "I've already repented, isn't that enough? Besides, it's a long way back there!" With the guilt weighing heavily on my shoulders, He persisted.

I've disappointed my Lord so many times in this life, and I wanted to be obedient, so I turned around! I must admit, though, that was one of the longest five miles I've ever driven!

Ephesians 4: 29-30, 32 (NKJV) says "Let no corrupt word proceed out of your mouth, but what is good for necessary edification, that it may impart grace to the hearers. And do not grieve the Holy Spirit by whom you were sealed for the day of redemption...and be kind to one another, tender-hearted, forgiving one another, even as God in Christ forgave you." It was very clear that I had indeed grieved the Holy Spirit with my tongue and actions. Now, because He had shown me mercy and grace, it was my turn to do the same.

As I stepped up to the counter, the young lady looked at me with a hardened suspicion. But who could blame her? I certainly couldn't! So, praying as I began, I said, "Ma'am, I am so sorry for the way I spoke to you a while ago. I had no right. Please forgive me. I also need you to know that Jesus loves you, and no matter what you're going through, He cares." Fighting back tears, she accepted my apology and simply said, "Thank you."

Dear reader, if you need to apologize today, don't hesitate! Life's too short to live with regret. If the one you've hurt is no longer here, take it to the Lord. 1 John 1:9 (NKJV) reminds us that "if we confess our sins, He is faithful and just to forgive us our sins and to cleanse us from all unrighteousness." If you confess, He'll handle the rest!

With others waiting behind me to place their order, our conversation was quick and to the point. However, it was evident that the Holy Spirit had done a work in both of us that day. But before I stepped away, I asked one more question — "Could you please make me a pot of fresh decaf?"

De

"For by grace you have been saved through faith, and not of yourselves, it is the gift of God, not of works, lest anyone should boast." Ephesians 2:8-9 (NKJV)

The Lord was leading me to share the Gospel with De (not her real name), and I didn't do it. There's no need to sugarcoat the situation — the Lord had clearly given me an assignment, and I failed.

I can't describe the anguish I felt when the call came telling me that she had passed away. A couple of days later, standing next to her casket, I wanted so badly to ask her, "De, are you in Hell today because I didn't tell you?!" The guilt was so heavy. I still live with the regret, today.

Now, I realize that I cannot save anyone! We are saved through faith alone, in Christ alone. In John 6:44a (NKJV), Jesus says, "No one can come to Me unless the Father who sent Me draws him." Then again in John 14:6 (NKJV), "I am the way, the truth, and the life. No one comes to the Father except through Me."

Jesus is the only one who can save a soul, but before He left this world to sit at the right hand of His Father, He left very clear instructions: "Go and tell!" Matthew 28:19-20, "Jesus was filled with compassion as He cast out demons, fed the hungry, and healed the sick." However, as I read Matthew 9:37-38 (NKJV), I can imagine an immense sadness in His voice as He looked out over those same people and said, "The harvest is truly plentiful, but the laborers are few. Therefore, pray the Lord of the harvest to send out laborers into His harvest."

People are no different today than they were in biblical times. Everywhere you look, souls are searching for hope and healing, and wanting someone, somewhere to care. I've been called to be one of the laborers. If you claim the name of Christ, so have you. We save no one, but we certainly can point them to the One who can save!

Charles Spurgeon said, "If sinners be damned, at least let them leap to Hell over our dead bodies. And if they perish, let them perish with our arms wrapped about their knees, imploring them to stay. If Hell must be filled, let it be filled in the teeth of our exertions, and let not one go unwarned and unprayed for." Lord, help me to be that bold.

I will forever regret not sharing the Good News with my friend. However, I must rest in God's sovereignty and trust that De was given an opportunity to accept Christ as her Savior. But until we stand before Him to give an account, I pray that both you and I, dear reader, will be obedient and bold in sharing the Gospel with whoever will listen.

Forgiving Her

"And forgive our debts, as we forgive our debtors."
- Matthew 6:11 (NKJV)

The sound check was done, and the song list was in place. After time spent in prayer, I felt confident in the Lord and ready to sing! It was going to be an exciting evening, and I was anticipating a move of God — that is, until "she" walked in.

My heart started to feel faint, and my knees were weak. Mental images and hurts from the past began flooding my soul and mind. I immediately began to cry out, "God, no! Why here, and why now?!" Just in case He didn't remember, I began going down my list of her offenses, and they weren't pretty! However, that still small voice of the Holy Spirit whispered, "It's okay, she's one of mine."

Even though twenty-plus years had passed, it was obvious that I still held unforgiveness in my heart towards this lady. It was a weight I hated, but still carried. In my mind, much of my past hurt was her fault. Little did I know that somewhere during those same years, she had given her heart to Christ and was now a new creation and my sister in the Lord. 2 Corinthians 5:17 (NKJV) says, "If anyone is in Christ, he is a new creation; old things have passed away, behold, all things have become new."

With the Holy Spirit's urging, I slowly made my way to where she was seated and extended my hand to say, "Hello". She was hesitant at first, but finally took hold. With a knowing smile, we were on the same path — I needed to forgive, and she needed closure. That night,

God met us there. I can't tell you anything about the concert itself, but the anticipation of His moving was more than I could have ever imagined.

As the service closed that evening, the pastor had everyone gather around the altar to pray. Only one or two in the congregation knew of our past, and I was thankful. But there we stood, side by side, praying and praising the One who loved us both equally and unconditionally. After the final amen was spoken, she turned to me and said, "I'm so sorry for everything." And what rolled off my tongue, yet came from deep within, were words only God could provide: "You're forgiven."

John R. Rice once said, "Unforgiveness is choosing to stay trapped in a jail cell of bitterness, serving time for someone else's crime." I found that to be true, but as I let go, the prison bars opened.

Friendship Baptist Church: He is Enough

The pastor was so excited! The church was filled almost to capacity, and the people were anticipating a mighty move of God! Even more exciting was seeing the first two rows on both sides of the sanctuary filled with teenagers! The problem was that, as the guest singer for the evening, I was not prepared. In fact, after my husband and I got the sound set and ready to go, I went into the restroom, locked the door, and began to weep uncontrollably. I was in that deep, dark hole called Clinical Depression, and no matter how hard I tried, I couldn't get out!

Trying to regain my composure, I prayed, "Lord, I can't do this! I know there's a church full of people out there expecting me to sing and testify, but all I want to do is get out of here, now!" However, with the service starting in no less than five minutes, I couldn't leave! Besides, I'm not one to walk out.

As I looked in the mirror to freshen up, I could see that my makeup was gone entirely, and it was not pretty! I was not pretty. I was a mess. But, I was God's mess and He was going to have to do something! And He did.

Looking back, I can't tell you any of the songs I sang or much of what was said. But one thing I CAN tell you is that God DID show up in a mighty way! The altar was packed that night with young and old alike doing business with Jesus! I'll never forget that moment in time for the rest of my life. To God be the glory!

I also learned a hard lesson that night. You see, God didn't have to have me there to pour out His Spirit — He's

God! He can use anything or anyone He chooses at any time to accomplish His will, for His glory! However, I firmly believe that He desires to use me! I am His workmanship, created in Christ Jesus for good works. (Ephesians 2:10) So that night, He chose to use me in my weakness to show just how strong He is.

My experience in that deep, dark hole lasted for about a year, and by God's grace, it has never returned. However, God used that moment in time to teach me to have more compassion and understanding for those who walk that road, since I was once where they are, now. But most importantly, I believe it taught me to grasp the full reality that when I am at my weakest, He shines the brightest.

The Lord said to Paul, "My grace is sufficient for you, for My strength is made perfect in weakness. Therefore, most gladly I will rather boast in my infirmities, that the power of Christ may rest upon me. Therefore, I take pleasure in infirmities, in reproaches, in needs, in persecutions, in distresses, for Christ's sake. For when I am weak, then I am strong." 2 Corinthians 12:9-10 (NKJV)

Dear reader, never forget — He is enough!

God, Are You Proud of Me?

"Have you considered my son, Job?" - Job 1:8b

Like a child that constantly needs reminding, I often find myself needing to hear my Savior tell me again and again just how much He loves me. Perhaps you need that reminder as well.

As the band took the field that day, it didn't take long to find my son. After all, there were only two bass drums in the drumline. It didn't matter to me that he was also the youngest or least experienced one out there, either! I was a proud mom, and oh, how I wanted to shout out and make sure everyone paid close attention—MY son was about to play! My heart was so full as the tears rolled down my face, and that's when the thought occurred to me. "God, do you look at me that way?"

I didn't hear an immediate response, but the question kept floating around in the back of my mind. I knew God loved me! His blessings were evident; all I had to do was look around. But still I wondered, was He "proud" of me? A few weeks later, the answer came.

In Job 1:8 (CSB) we read, "Then the Lord said to Satan, 'Have you considered my servant Job? No one else on earth is like him, a man of perfect integrity, who fears God and turns away from evil.'"

I have no intention of taking the verse or the account of Job out of context, but the moment I read those words, the question I had asked God, suddenly moved to the front of my mind as the Holy Spirit answered me and said, "Yes, child, I certainly look at you that way, and I am proud of you!" Although Job was about to be tested beyond what you and I can imagine, I can hear the pride in the Father's heart as He said, "That's my child! You'd better pay attention!"

In this great big world, we often feel so small — and we are! In the vastness of eternity, from the beginning to forever, the Bible says that our life on this earth is but a vapor. (James 4:14) However, no child of God should ever lose sight of the fact that He sees and loves you! The One who created it all created you on purpose, for a purpose!

David also reminds us in Psalms 139:17, "How precious are your thoughts to me, O God! How great the sum of them!"

Dear reader, you don't have to be playing in the band, standing on the stage, or performing some huge task for your Father to be proud of you. Did you speak a word of encouragement to a friend? Did you offer a helping hand to a neighbor in need? Did you spend time with Him in prayer interceding for someone He laid on your heart? Did you earnestly seek Him through His Word today? All He asks is faithfulness and obedience for the task at hand.

This little devotion may not be for everyone. But if you are asking, like I did, "God, do you look at me that way?" The answer to you is this. "Yes, my child, yes. You're mine and I am so proud!"

God's Great Love

"Greater love has no one than this..."-John 15:13

God's love—no matter how hard I try, I can't seem to wrap my mind around it! All my life, I've been told about it, read about it, and even sung about it! I've seen it at work in so many lives around me, and I rejoice! Most importantly, I experienced it firsthand by faith when Jesus saved my soul.

In my flesh, the closest thing with which I can compare God's love is the love I have for my own children. I would lay down everything I have, even my own life, so that they could live! Yet, I realize this deep, unconditional, passionate, and fierce mother's love is absolutely nothing compared to God's love for me—or for you.

As Jesus hung on the cross, stretched between Heaven and Earth, He paid the full penalty for my sin. It should have been me on that cross, but because of His love, He took my place! Try as I may, I can't fathom all He went through.

He was broken, slaughtered, and sacrificed for me! He was stripped naked, spit upon, mocked, and beaten beyond recognition, while a crown of thorns was shoved onto His head! But because of His perfect love, He said, "Father, forgive them, for they do not know what they do." Luke 23:34 (NKJV)

If someone stood before me with the blood of my child on their hands, in my flesh, I must admit that I would want nothing more than justice and revenge! And yet, before He saved me, I stood guilty of that very sin, killing the only Son of God! My mind cannot conceive this!

Jesus took God's wrath for my sin upon Himself! Who can grasp a love so pure? This side of Heaven, no word ever spoken or song ever sung, will completely capture its depth. Yet because of this perfect love, the Lord offers Himself freely to "whoever believes" — and by faith, I do!

"For God so loved the world that He gave His only begotten Son, that whoever believes in Him should not perish but have everlasting life." John 3:16 (NKJV)

My attempt to understand this Love is so feeble, yet pondering it causes me to fall to the ground in worship and cry out praises for His love to me! "For now we see only a reflection as in a mirror, but then face to face. Now I know in part, but then I will know fully, as I am fully known." - 1 Corinthians 13:12 (CSB)

So today, even though I don't understand, I still rest in the full assurance knowing that He loved, so He gave — and one day soon, I'll understand.

Grandma

"...that you may know that you have eternal life." - 1 John 5:13b

  I never understood what was meant when I heard others speak of the "death rattles." But, as I stepped into her room that morning, I knew in an instant what the sound was.

  As my 102-year-old grandmother lay there, I knew that very soon, she would be stepping into eternity. Each labored breath took her one step closer to that moment when she would stand face-to-face, before Jesus.

  By early afternoon, certain family members had said their goodbyes so they could tend to their loved ones at home. Others could have been there, but chose not to, as grandma had pushed them away with her harshness and divisive attitude. My father and I stayed by her side until she left us. Now, believe me, I'm no super saint, as we had our issues, but she was still my grandma, and I loved her! I didn't want her to die alone.

  After she drew her last breath, I touched her face and said, "Oh, grandma! What do you see?! What do you hear?!" My troubled heart searched her face, looking for any indication that she was at peace and all was well. I saw no signs of happiness or tense expressions telling me of her final destination. She looked as if she were asleep, but I knew she was gone. I'm still not certain where she's spending eternity, and my heart breaks at this thought. I know, however, that God is trustworthy, and He has it all under control.

  Her body now removed, I looked around the empty

room, shaking my head. The only sign that another life had even been there were a few personal items and other things that would now be passed on to other patients.

My heart was hurting as I tried not to cry. Looking at my father, I said in a half-way, sarcastic tone, "So, this is it? One hundred and two years, and the books are closed? Now all that's left to show for her life are a few lousy cards, pictures, and some stale cookies. No more second chances, and no more opportunities to say I'm sorry or I love you. And the worst part of all, I don't know where she is!" That's when I broke.

It has been said that "Wounded people, wound people." My grandmother hurt many along the way, including me, with her harsh words and attitude. Matthew 12:34b tells us that, "...out of the abundance of the heart, the mouth speaks." I've often wondered what deep, open wound lay within my grandmother's heart that caused her to speak so sharply and act the way she sometimes did.

Many times, when it was just Grandma and me, I would press her about her relationship with Christ. I wanted to know when she was saved! However, she always took me to the day she was baptized. The best I could gather was that a revival was taking place, and she and two of her sisters were possibly saved and baptized on the same day. The creek wasn't far from the church, so that made sense.

But something was missing. As her health began to deteriorate, I asked on more than one occasion if she was indeed ready to meet the Lord. Her response was always "Oh, I think so." Perhaps you can understand why I'm not certain where her soul is today.

What about you, dear reader? Do you know for sure where you'll spend eternity? You can be! Ephesians 2:8-9 (NKJV) says, "For by grace you have been saved, through faith, and that not of yourselves; it is the gift of

God, not of works, lest anyone should boast."

And if you're not sure about your salvation, the entire book of I John was written, "…that you may know that you have eternal life, and that you may continue to believe in the name of the Son of God." - I John 5:13b (NKJV)

It's only by faith in the One, Jesus Christ, who paid the ultimate sacrifice for you to have eternal life. In John 3:3 (NKJV), Jesus said, "Most assuredly, I say to you, unless one is born again, he cannot see the kingdom of God."

What about you? Are you ready?

Grandpa Tony

"...I will come again and receive you to Myself; that where I am, there you may be also." - John 14:3 (NKJV)

For the past few weeks, I've been homesick for my grandfather. There's nothing special about this time of year that would cause such an emotion; I simply miss him. And, even though it has been well over twenty years since the Lord called him home, there are days I can still hear his voice.

He was the kind of grandpa who thought it was important to teach my cousins and me the fine art of fishing, even though I still refuse to bait my own hook! On top of that are the precious memories of backyard softball and ending the day with tales of "The Three Billy Goats Gruff." I also remember the day I stood quietly beside him during worship so that I could hear him sing. He was by no means perfect, but he was my grandpa, and I loved him! I also know that he loved me.

The day he left us, God intervened in so many ways. Perhaps at some point I'll be able to share them with you. But the most bittersweet memory of that day is when, just moments before he stepped into eternity, I was given the opportunity to look into his sweet face one last time and ask, "Grandpa, are you ready to meet the Lord? I need to know for sure!" He turned his head my way, gave me an assuring nod, and said, "Yes, I'm ready." Less than an hour later, he closed his eyes to this world only to open them and see the sweet face of Jesus!

I left the hospital that night holding the old wooden

cane he had to use to stand or walk. It now leans against a corner in my home, a reminder that he doesn't need it anymore. He's completely healed! In my mind's eye, I can see him running down that golden street, praising the Lord.

1 Thessalonians 4:13-14, 16-18 (NKJV) says, "But I do not want you to be ignorant, brethren, concerning those who have fallen asleep (died) lest you sorrow as others who have no hope. For if we believe that Jesus died and rose again, even so God will bring with Him those who sleep in Jesus…For the Lord Himself will descend from heaven with a shout, with the voice of an archangel and with the trumpet of God. And the dead in Christ will rise first. Then we who are alive and remain shall be caught up together with them in the clouds to meet the Lord in the air. And thus we shall always be with the Lord. Therefore, comfort one another with these words." Oh, what a comfort it is!

A song I recorded recently makes me long for that day Paul describes in this passage. The chorus says:
"One Day Soon, we'll be united,
One Day Soon, we'll meet again,
One Day Soon, we'll live forever,
And sing a song that never ends….
We'll sing a song that never ends!"

On that day, I won't have to stand quietly beside Grandpa to listen. We'll sing together, praising the One who loves us both! Will you be joining us?

— — — — — —

"One Day Soon" was written by Dixie Phillips and Matthew Lawson.

Happy Birthday

"For whoever calls on the name of the LORD shall be saved."
- Romans 10:13 (NKJV)

Happy Birthday to me! I actually have two birthdays to celebrate during the month of June. One birthday, I'll smile and say thank you for the well wishes, as I'm not too thrilled with the number that is attached to it! Life truly is a vapor! (James 4:14)

It seems that only yesterday I was daydreaming of reaching the wise old age of being a teenager. Today, a not-so-wise teen can glance at me and know that I'm eligible for a senior coffee! That "vapor stuff" happens just way too fast! However, the second birthday I'm celebrating this month is for when I was re-born, and I became a child of God! Or as we like to say, "I got saved!"

I don't remember the exact date. I can tell you, however, where I was sitting in our little church and what I was wearing that Thursday evening in June. I don't remember much of the message, but the Holy Spirit grabbed my young heart that night, and I knew I needed a Savior! I didn't look to my parents for permission; I just left my seat and headed straight for my pastor. In his gentle way, he led me to the Throne of Grace, and that night, my life was changed forever.

Over these fifty-plus years, walking with the Lord, I must admit that I have failed Him so often. But when I truly repent, He's always faithful to forgive. (1 John 1:9) Yes, there have been consequences for my sin, but since He's my Father, His love has never let me go. Nothing can separate me from a love that is perfect and unconditional. (Romans 8:38).

I've also faced some deep, dark valleys and cried bitter tears while I wondered if the open wounds to my heart would ever heal. But just as He's promised in Psalms 147:3, He bandaged my wounds and healed my broken heart. Today I stand, not on my own two feet, but because of His strong arms that hold me up. However, far and above my failures and tragedies, one thing is sure. I know beyond a shadow of a doubt that I am a child of God. (1 John 3:1) My Heavenly Daddy is the Creator and King over everything. I am a Princess in the courts of the King, and one day He'll take me home and I'll live with him forever! I am blessed.

For you see, dear reader, I can truly testify that I've been saved by grace, through faith in Jesus Christ and not of myself; God offered this gift of salvation to me. There's nothing that I could ever do to earn it, as I have nothing to boast about. (Ephesians 2:8-9) And for this gift, I will celebrate!

What's even more exciting is that this gift is for anyone willing to reach out and accept it! It's right there with your name written on it. I can see the card—it says "To: Whosoever will, Love, Jesus." Will you accept it?

Just Passing Through

Jesus said, "Whoever receives one little child like this in my name receives Me. Whoever causes one of these little ones who believe in Me to sin, it would be better for him if a millstone were hung around his neck, and he were drowned in the depth of the sea."- Matthew 18:5-6

I wasn't begging for attention when I walked in that Sunday morning; I was just a visitor passing through. Not needing to be at my concert venue until late afternoon, I was so excited to be a part of the congregation and worship with brothers and sisters that I had never met! However, the coldness I experienced left me confused. Then it convicted me.

Walking into the church, I was met with suspicion as one of the two greeters handed me a bulletin. They were cordial, but that's as far as it went. I asked if it was okay to sit in the sanctuary until worship began. With hesitation in their voices, they gave me permission, but made sure I knew to be quiet as there was a Bible study going on. Feeling like a child that had just been scolded, I quickly found a seat, hoping I wouldn't be accused of taking someone's pew.

As the study dismissed and the sanctuary filled, I started to feel out of place. I didn't expect everyone to rush over and grab me with a holy hug, but a simple nod or handshake to say "hello" would have been nice!

Within a few minutes, people were sitting all around me. The room was filled with noise, yet the silence in my heart and mind was deafening!

The service began with a song by the choir that

said something about Jesus being welcome, and in my smugness, I told myself that the Lord didn't believe one word they were singing!

After the final amen, chatter once again filled the room, and shoulder-to-shoulder we made our way to the exit. Now, if you know me, you know that I have no problem talking to strangers. I really did try to engage with some of those people, but no one seemed interested. This was a concept I simply couldn't understand.

However, the Lord was about to teach me a lesson that I will never forget. Just as I reached the door, I heard a voice over the noise of the crowd from somewhere behind me holler, "Ma'am, Ma'am!" As I turned, a lady was reaching over three or four others, trying to grab my shoulder to get my attention. When we made eye contact, she said, "We're so glad you're here!" I waved and said, "Thank you!" And just like that, she was gone. "Thank you, Lord."

That afternoon, I replayed the morning's episode over and over in my mind. Every time I tried to judge their unfriendly actions and justify my response, conviction came. When I pointed one finger at them, three pointed back at me, reminding me of the times I walked on by without a smile or a simple handshake of welcome. "Forgive me, Lord."

The Holy Spirit continues to use that day as a reminder that we all need to pay more attention to who walks through the doors of the church. It may be someone just passing through like I was, and all it takes is two steps across the aisle, joined with a smile and a simple handshake to bless their day.

And yet, while the above is true, it goes even deeper. I have a question that has haunted me ever since that day. What if I had not been just passing through? What if, when I walked through those doors, I was searching for some peace, only to be ignored? What if I had heard something about this Jesus, wanting to know more, yet walked out of the building with no one extending His hand to me?

What if someone walks through the doors of your church this Sunday searching for peace and forgiveness? Will they find it there? Oh, how I want the Lord to use me like He did that little lady who pressed through the crowd to touch my shoulder and say, "We're glad you're here!" What about you? Will you be the one He uses?

Yes, we must reach outside the four walls of the church building, but maybe that "love thy neighbor" is only a handshake away.

No More Excuses

As far back as I can remember, all I ever wanted to do was sing a song! I couldn't have been more than four years old when my babysitter stood me on a stoop at her church picnic and said, "Sing!" So I did! However, I was well into my twenties before I realized that God had placed that desire inside of me as a tool to fulfill a calling He had for my life.

Whether I was singing the melody line or filling in the harmonies, most of it came easily, and I was comfortable. However, comfort is not where God desires His children to stay. Over the last forty-plus years of ministry, He has stretched and pulled me out of my comfort zone in ways I never thought possible. And, I assure you, each time He has called me to something more, I've used every excuse I could think of. Like you, I enjoy being comfortable!

I'm reminded that after Moses had fled from Egypt and the wrath of Pharaoh, Exodus 2:21 says that he was "content." Life was good, and he could relax! But God had bigger plans, and Moses's life was about to be forever changed. If you read a bit further in Exodus, God appeared and proved Himself in a mighty way when He told Moses that He had chosen him to lead His people out of bondage. God performed all sorts of signs and wonders, and yet Moses gave every excuse He could think of to get out of the job!

Exodus 4:10, 13 (NKJV)
Then Moses said to the Lord, "O my Lord, I am not

eloquent, neither before nor since You have spoken to Your servant: but I am slow of speech and slow of tongue." "O my Lord, please send by the hand of whomever else you may send."

It's so easy to look at Moses and point a finger in judgment. God had proven Himself many times over, and yet Moses still made excuses as to why he couldn't, or shouldn't, be God's spokesman. I remember making the very same excuses as Moses, plus a few more, when God called me deeper into ministry. Answering the call can be hard—ask Moses! Jesus said it would be! (John 16:33) But our mandate is clear. As He was ascending into Heaven, He said, "Go...." He then made a promise, "...I am with you always." (Matthew 28:19-20) There is a lost and dying world out there, and God wants to use you to bring them in!

What about you, dear reader? What is God calling you to? If God can take this little girl from out of the middle of nowhere and place His mark on her for His service and glory (which He did), He can—and wants—to use you. No more running; no more excuses.

Remember this: God doesn't always call the qualified, but He WILL qualify the called!

Speed It Up

"I will send down showers in their season; they will be showers of blessing." - Ezekiel 34:26b

I'll never forget the "death stare" we received that Sunday morning during worship service. If one of our parents had realized what was going on, they would have "nipped it in the bud" that very moment in front of God and everyone present! But since we were both about thirteen years old, looking for permission never crossed our minds. Besides, we knew how this particular song was supposed to go, and she was messing it up!

Mrs. Gervin was a quiet, prim, and proper white-haired lady who faithfully played the organ each week for our congregation. I'm sure she was professionally trained in this fine art, but my friend and I had had enough! It seemed as if the older this sophisticated lady became, the slower the music got! On this particular day, we were tired of singing "Count Your Many Blessings" as if we were in some death march, so we did what any intelligent, well-informed teenager would do — we tried to speed it up!

By the time we reached the chorus, we were at least four measures ahead and thought our version sounded great! However, no one else was willing to join in our little revolt. After the death stare had been fired our way and others began to notice something wasn't quite right, we dutifully fell back in line.

Today, I still enjoy singing that song with gusto! The blessings that God has poured over me cause me to rejoice! However, could it be that Mrs. Gervin knew something deep in her soul that this childish teenager and her friend had yet to learn?

Count Your Blessings
1. *When upon life's billows you are tempest tossed; When you are discouraged thinking all is lost. Count your many blessings name them one by one; And it will surprise you what the Lord hath done.*
Chorus
Count your blessings, name them one by one; Count your blessings, see what God has done.... *

    Dark days fall upon even those who are in Christ; we know that. But even then, God's blessings are still there. Count them one by one. You'll see that the well is full, and it is deep.
    Ephesians 1:3 (NIV) says, "Praise be to the God and Father of our Lord Jesus Christ, who has blessed us in the heavenly realms with every spiritual blessing in Christ!"
    If apologies are given in Heaven, I'll make sure to give Mrs. Gervin mine. Perhaps then I'll hear all about those blessings and why she insisted on playing that song so slow. But until then, clap your hands and sing!
"Count your Blessings, name them one by one..."

---

*Count Your Blessings" written by Johnson Oatman, Jr., 1897.

The Blessings of Brokenness

"Your Word is a lamp to my feet and a light to my path."
- Psalm 119:105

My life was already falling apart with fear and uncertainty, but on that cold day in February of 1987, reality set in — my nine-year marriage was over. With no marketable job skills, no place to live, and a young child to care for, the only choice I had was to move back home with my parents. I felt alone, ashamed, and humiliated. I was broken.

With precise accuracy, the shots fired by the enemy seemed to hit every target area of my heart. Words like unlovable, ugly, fat, worthless, and stupid never left me. Even as a Born-Again Believer, I bought into the lie that said, "God could never use me again". Deep inside of me, however, buried underneath all of the despair, a seed had been planted many years earlier by the One who loved me more than any man, woman, or child ever could; my Lord and Savior, Jesus Christ.

A few weeks after moving back home, my mother bought me a new Bible, which became my lifeline. From its pages, the Holy Spirit began to water and nourish the seed buried deep within me. Little by little, hope for the future began to blossom. I can still tell you today, the exact spot I was sitting when Ephesians 3:20-21 flooded my dry soul, "Now to Him who is able to do exceedingly, abundantly above all that we ask or think, according to the power that works in us, to Him be glory in the church by Christ Jesus throughout all ages, world without end,

Amen".

Also underlined and highlighted is Psalm 27:13-14 that says, "I would have lost heart, unless I had believed that I would see the goodness of the LORD in the land of the living. Wait on the LORD; Be of good courage, and He shall strengthen your heart; Wait, I say, on the LORD!

Dear reader, I don't know where you are or what you're walking through, and that's OK — God does! Never forget that He loves you and His promises are sure.

My path to healing wasn't easy or overnight — it was a minute-by-minute and day-by-day process. But, I can certainly testify that He has done "Exceedingly, abundantly above all I could ever ask or think..." and He can do the same for you.

Today, that Bible has a special spot on my bookcase, as its pages are worn and barely holding together. I now have others that have replaced it as my study source, but on occasion, I'll pull it out for reference or to simply remember. For you see, in its pages, the Lord proved to me that yes, I am loved and adored. He also proved that my worth was so great that He sent His only Son to die for me.

I still have trials; in fact, I'm there right now. But I will forever hold on to the promise that says, "He'll never leave or forsake me." (Hebrews 13:5)

The T-Shirt

"...and grant to Your servants that with all boldness they may speak Your word..." - Acts 4:29

Like most dedicated Christians, I've always believed that when the time came to stand firm on the side of a truth, I would have no problem doing so! Recently, however, the Lord showed me that I was not as bold as I had claimed to be. Some would have called me a hypocrite. And quite possibly, they would have been correct.

A few months ago, I purchased a t-shirt that has the words "Babies Lives Matter" printed in large letters on the front. Anxious to take my bold, pro-life stand, I wore the shirt one evening to church, as I worked in the kitchen for the children's program. Now, if you skimmed over that last sentence, read it again. Little did I know that the Lord was about to show me just how bold I was.

While out running errands, I dress a bit nicer than just jeans and a t-shirt. In fact, on this particular day, I had the perfect outfit already chosen! But, as I was getting dressed, the Holy Spirit's still small voice began to speak, prompting me to wear "The Shirt." I tried convincing Him that the outfit I had picked out was much more appropriate! Besides, I didn't want to cause any unnecessary outbursts with its bold message! I'm sure that you, dear reader, have never argued with the Lord.

In the 22nd chapter of Luke, Peter arrogantly said, "Lord, I am ready to go with You both to prison and to death!" (v. 33). Could it be that, like me, Peter DID believe he was that strong? I wonder if it made him angry when Jesus immediately said, "I tell you Peter, the rooster shall not crow this day before you will deny three times that you know Me." (v. 34) His angry arrogance soon turned into deep grief when he realized that he had done the very thing he said he would not do — deny he even knew Jesus. (vv. 57-60)   Praise the Lord, after that failure, Peter was filled with boldness, leading the way as the church grew. Read the entire book of Acts!

As I write this, I'm also reminded of the boldness of Stephen in chapter seven of Acts. Until his death, he remained steadfast in his faith while sharing the Gospel of Christ. As the stones were being thrown to kill him, he never backed down. And just before he took his final breath, he said, "Lord, do not charge them with this sin." Acts 7:60 (NKJV) This causes me to hang my head in shame.

I must admit to you that standing on a stage singing a Gospel song or speaking at a ladies' event in front of crowds of people is easier for me than talking to people one-on-one. Most of the time, I'm with people like me who also believe like me. It's when I'm out and away from the safety of those people that life runs into my beliefs, and my faith is put to the test.

God knew that I needed to see the cowardly hypocrite I was that day. Looking into His mirror, I quickly realized this had nothing to do with the shirt itself, but a heart problem that I didn't want to see. I wasn't as bold as I claimed to be. With conviction quickly coming over me, I cried out for forgiveness and asked the Lord to give me the boldness I so desperately needed.

Believers around the world still give their very lives for the cause of Christ. There may come a day when you and I have to face the very same fate. It makes my t-shirt fiasco seem so trivial, yet it was a lesson I needed to be taught.

Influence

My sweet husband was waiting up for me that late Sunday evening; I had been gone for several days, presenting a couple of concerts and speaking at a ladies' retreat. After I settled in, he was eager to hear how everything had gone, and I was eager to share! I began rattling off some of the exciting things that God had done, when a thought suddenly stopped me mid-sentence. It was then that I realized that even though I had just experienced some remarkable things in the Lord, under my very roof were the ones I had been called to minister to first.

Upstairs, asleep, were my two precious children who went to bed believing that Mom would be home when they woke the next morning. Sitting up in bed was my husband, who had anxiously awaited my return. In that moment of sudden realization, I looked into the face of my sweet man and said, "You know, none of that's important. What I need to know is this: "Do you believe that I'm real? Do the kids believe that I'm real?" With a questioning look on his face, I continued. "Do you and they know that I don't sing and speak just for fun, but that I REALLY love Jesus and am called to this ministry?"

Mark 8:36 (KJV) says, "For what shall it profit a man, if he shall gain the whole world and lose his own soul?" While that is true, what about this question: What shall it profit if I stay busy doing good things in the name of Jesus, yet neglect the greatest mission field right in front of me?

When God calls us to ministry, we need to respond

and go! If we don't answer the call, we'll be miserable until we do. Trust me, I know that for a fact! But as you and I go, may we never forget the precious gift of those closest to us that He has also called us to minister to first.

My Greatest Fear

Right there before God, the Pastor, a Tennessee State Senator and a couple of others in the sanctuary, my pride took a nosedive. Stepping upon the podium to do a Facebook live concert, I fell! It wasn't a very ladylike tumble either. Fortunately, the camera had yet to start filming and only those in the room witnessed my embarrassment.

By the time I returned to my motel, I could barely walk. What had started out as a golf ball-sized knot was now a huge bruise that extended from the bottom of my foot to halfway up the calf of my leg.

I've often been asked if I'm ever frightened when standing before an audience. Jokingly, I always reply that my two greatest fears are stepping onto the podium with the hem of my skirt tucked where it's not supposed to be and/or falling off of said podium.

Many times before the above incident, I've come close to doing both! However, I have a far greater fear - I'm afraid of walking through a door that God has opened, only to find that I've put myself on center stage while claiming a glory that belongs to Him alone. I know the shame, regret, and loss of blessings that occur because I've done it more than once. I'm sure you have as well. In Proverbs 11:2 (NKJV), we read, "When pride comes, then comes shame; But with the humble is wisdom."

Also, in Proverbs 16:18 (NKJV), "Pride goes before destruction, and a haughty spirit before a fall." I'm so thankful for two words- But God! For you see, every time I fall, because I'm His child, the Holy Spirit steps in with correction, love, and grace. Proverbs 3:11-12 (NAS) says,

"My son, do not reject the discipline of the LORD or loathe His reproof, For whom the LORD loves, He reproves, Even as a father corrects the son in whom he delights."

The following Scripture is my heart's cry for every day He gives me. I pray, dear reader, it is for you as well.

Psalm 19:13-15 (NKJV)
"Keep back Your servant also from presumptuous sins; Let them not have dominion over me. Then I shall be blameless, and I shall be innocent of great transgression. Let the words of my mouth and the meditation of my heart Be acceptable in Your sight, O Lord, my strength and my Redeemer."

Now, back to my fear of a possible wardrobe malfunction - if we're ever in the same place at the same time and you notice something not quite right, I would appreciate a nod in my direction.

Hold Me

My father was the only one home that summer day as I ran through the front door. I melted into a pool of tears, and the only words I could muster were, "Oh, Daddy!" My broken heart and life had taken yet another blow that caused me to wonder if I could, or ever would, recover.

Making my way to the back of the house, I curled up on the bed and continued to weep. Without saying a word, he followed me, hoping to offer some sort of comfort. Even though I was a grown adult, I was still his child needing support that could only come from a loving parent. So in that moment, my daddy did the only thing he knew to do – he lay down beside me, wrapped his arms around me, and cried too.

That bittersweet day will be forever etched in my mind. While I was engulfed in a sea of fear, anger, shame, and complete brokenness, my father displayed grace, love, and mercy over me. Through it all, not one time did He ever speak words of condemnation or judgment. However, because he's my earthly father, there was only so much he could do to ease the pain and heal my wounds. I needed a touch from the One who loved me perfectly and loved me BEYOND my dad's love, and that was my Heavenly Father!

As I read Psalm 40:1-3, 16 (NKJV), I'm reminded of the grace and mercy He has lavishly poured on me throughout my life. And dear reader, if you're in Christ, the same is true for you.

1. I waited patiently for the Lord, and He inclined to me

and heard my cry.
2. He also brought me up out of a horrible pit, out of the miry clay and set my feet upon a rock, and established my steps.
3. He has put a new song in my mouth - Praise to our God; many will see it and fear and will trust in the LORD.
16. Let all those who seek You rejoice and be glad in You; Let such as love Your salvation say continually, "The LORD be magnified!"

    My healing didn't come over-night. In fact, I won't receive my complete healing until Jesus takes me to my eternal home. Until then, I carry the scars that are only a reminder of where I was and Who it is that carries me through. But as I go, I will sing that new song He has put in my mouth with PRAISE!

Audience of One

To help kick off the season, I was invited to emcee and share a couple of songs for a community Christmas program that my daughter was overseeing. Excitement and nervous jitters filled the air as family and friends gathered in the auditorium while performers prepared for an afternoon of music and fun.

As the lights lowered and the music began, I boldly walked onto the stage to welcome the crowd and sing the opening song. However, that same boldness quickly disappeared as the bright spotlight zeroed in on me. Almost blinded, I was unable to see anyone sitting in the auditorium! But, with the music playing, I had no choice but to sing! I knew the people were there, but it seemed my only audience was that ONE LIGHT.

I moved around, trying to cover my nervousness and engage people I could not see, but the light followed my every move. I could see no smiles or frowns that would indicate if the performance was good or bad. And to top it all off, I felt as if everything wrong with me was being highlighted – from the wrinkles on my face, to my gray roots that were in desperate need of color, right down to the snags on my hose. That ONE LIGHT caused me to feel vulnerable, small, and weak.

Later, alone with my thoughts, I was quickly reminded of the calling that had been placed on my life by the Lord. No matter how large or small the crowd, or how good or bad the response, I should be concerned only with the audience of the One Light I sing to and for! It is Christ, my Savior that I am to please. Admittedly, I don't always get it right.

I'm also reminded that one day we must all appear before the Judgment Seat of Christ so that each may be repaid for what he has done in the body, whether good or evil. (2 Corinthians 5:9-10) As we stand before that audience of One, nothing will be hidden. What a sobering thought! "Therefore, God also has highly exalted Him and given Him the name which is above every name, that at the name of Jesus every knee should bow, of those in heaven and of those on the earth, and of those under the earth, and that every tongue should confess the Jesus Christ is Lord to the glory of God the Father." - Philippians 2: 9-11 (NKJV)

May you and I never forget to focus on the true Light. Jesus said, "I am the light of the world. He who follows Me shall not walk in darkness but have the light of life." - John 8:12 (NKJV) Our audience of One.

Lift Up Those Shackled Arms!

Do you ever get aggravated with yourself? I most certainly do! Lately, there have been days that I've pictured the Lord looking at me with an exasperated expression on His face, totally speechless because I've let worry and doubt creep in. He's taken me to task more than once, whispering a question in my heart: "Cheri, do you really believe the message in those songs you sing?" My answer is, of course, "Yes, Lord! You know I do!" To which He said, "Then why aren't you living like you do!?" Maybe that's why He keeps taking me back to the book of Philippians.

So often I've been guilty of reading a passage without considering the situation or emotion tied to it. There are days I forget that the men God used to write His love letter to the world walked, talked, laughed, and cried just like you and me! They understood firsthand what it meant to suffer for the cause of Christ. And most of them died because of their stand for His truth. Then there's me, fretting over the "what ifs." Father, forgive me.

Chained in prison for sharing the Gospel, Paul still praised the Lord while writing messages of hope and encouragement to his brothers and sisters in the faith. In my mind's eye, I can see him placing his hands square on someone's shoulders as he intently looks into their eyes, saying, "Let it soak in. The Lord is with us! It's not over until HE says it's over! Now, let's PRAISE HIM!" I then imagine watching the tears flow down his face, hearing the cry in his voice as he raises those shackled arms toward heaven and shouts, "Rejoice in the Lord always! Again, I will say, rejoice! Let your gentleness be known unto all men. The LORD is at hand! Be anxious for nothing; but in everything by prayer and supplication with thanksgiving, let your requests be made known unto God; And the peace of God, which surpasses all understanding, will guard your hearts and minds through Christ Jesus. Finally, brethren, whatever things are true, whatever things are noble, whatever things are just, whatever things are pure, whatever things are lovely, whatever things are of good report; if there is any virtue, and if there is anything praiseworthy - meditate on these things. The things, which you learned, and received, and heard, and saw in me, these do, and the God of peace will be with you." Philippians 4:4-9 (NKJV)

    The Lord understands our weaknesses and also encourages us to cry out in our distress. 1 Peter 5:7 tells us to, "cast all [our] cares upon Him, for He cares for [us]!" He also understands the battle we fight every single day! But, oh dear reader, aren't you thankful for the peace that the Lord will bring to our troubled souls when we rest upon His promises.

No Mic Needed

"For My thoughts are not your thoughts, and My ways are not your ways. For as heaven is higher than the earth, so my ways are higher than your ways." - Isaiah 55: 8-9 (CSB)

When the Lord called me to leave my job for full-time ministry, I must admit that I had visions of grandeur! At this point, He had already expanded my territory through the music. Opportunities to speak at ladies' retreats, conferences, and banquets were also beginning to open up. I was excited, busy, and on my way—but to where? Little did I know that He was sending me on a journey where I would discover first-hand that, indeed, His thoughts are not my thoughts. During the months that I've been sharing my "Heart Thoughts" with you, I often feel like a broken record. More than once, I've said something to the effect that, "Often, true ministry isn't lived out on the public stage, but in the everyday things of life." It seems to be a statement the Lord has to keep firing back at me when my "visions of grandeur" continually get in the way.

Over the course of the last few days, this precept has become so clear as I've lived my own everyday life. First, I received a message from one asking for prayer, and then a phone call from another just needing someone to listen without judgment.

I've also been with one who is overwhelmed and stressed with work, and all it took was a couple of extra hands to help ease the load. All of this was done without a public stage and a mic in my hand.

I hope you can hear my heart through this written word. I don't say this to brag; it's life, and when the Spirit of God leads through it, it's ministry!

I also found one other who was in desperate need of being ministered to—me. Besides my Lord and then my husband, I have a few people close to me who know me without the dress and makeup. They sense when I'm down and in need of an encouraging word. They pray for me while I'm on and off the stage. They simply take time. I know they love me, and I am so blessed!

This week the Lord used a precious soul to be more of an encouragement and friend than she realized. Just by being there to share a very special moment while I sang two simple songs, her encouragement will never be forgotten. She had no stage or mic, as none was needed. It was just true, one-on-one ministry.

I wonder; could this be a part of what the apostle Paul meant when he said in Galatians 6:2 that we're to "Bear one another's burdens, and so fulfill the law of Christ?" I believe so.

There's not enough room in this simple entry to list the many ways in which we can help others to carry their loads. However, fulfilling the law of Christ can only be done one way—by loving one another. Jesus was serious when He said that we are to "love thy neighbor as thyself." That's exactly what my friend did when she gave up her time for me.

So indeed, His thoughts are not my thoughts, and the "higher ways and visions of grandeur" I often fight are simple rubbish compared to His ways. Yes, there are days that He does use me as I stand on a platform with a mic in my hand. However, more often than not, I experience His best work as I allow Him to love through me, one person at a time.

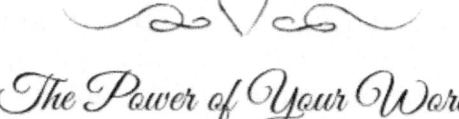

The Power of Your Words

"Words kill, words give life; they're either poison or fruit – you choose." - Proverbs 18:21 (MSG)

"Cross-eyed Freak" was the name I remember him calling me the most. His taunts were never loud enough for my friends to hear, but his whispers, when casually walking by, screamed right into my heart. Oh, how I wanted revenge! It took years for me to understand why he spoke as he did. Today, my heart breaks for that little boy. Why? Because when I look in the mirror, I see someone who's just as capable of causing an even deeper wound than the ones he inflicted on me.

I've jokingly said, "I'm usually hopping around on one foot because I'm always trying to get the other one out of my mouth!" Yes, we can laugh and have a good time! Proverbs 17:22a says, "A merry heart does good, like medicine!" But oh, how reckless you and I can be sometimes! A careless word here, a wrong tone used there, a confidence broken, or a bit of gossip passed on in fun can do so much damage, sometimes ruining lives forever!

When I was in high school, I received word about a horrible lie that had been told about me. Needless to say, I was devastated! Fortunately, when my friends and family realized the tale's source, it quickly died.

Many years later, I witnessed a look of hurt that pierced my own son's heart as the wrong words flew off my tongue. Although I earnestly apologized, my mother's heart will never forget the pain in his eyes and on his face.

How frightening it is to realize the power we hold to mortally wound someone's spirit simply by the words we speak! "…For out of the abundance of the heart the mouth speaks. ...I say to you that for every idle word men may speak, they will give an account of it in the day of judgment. For by your words you will be justified, and by your words you will be condemned." Matthew 12:34b, 36-37 (NKJV). God takes our words seriously, and we should too. If we claim the name of Christ and at the same time let words fly carelessly in the wind, we not only hurt others, but we also damage our own integrity and reputation. Is it any wonder that the world calls us hypocrites? Shame on us! Shame on me! I feel like the apostle Paul when he cried in Romans 3:7, "O wretched man I am! Who will rescue me from this body of death?" The answer? "But thanks be to God, who gives us the victory through our Lord Jesus Christ. (1 Cor. 15:57) I'm so thankful for grace.

    I don't know what became of that little boy from so long ago, or if he cares or not that I've forgiven him. Perhaps one day the Lord will give me the opportunity to ask his forgiveness for holding that grudge for so long.

VBS Bus Driver

Having once been a School Bus Driver, my pastor thought I'd be the perfect fit to transport some of the local children to and from Vacation Bible School (VBS) in the church van. Compared to driving a sixty-two passenger bus for an entire school year, a fifteen passenger van with a few children for one week would be a piece of cake - or so I thought! By the end of Wednesday's program, my nerves were frazzled, and my Jesus light was starting to dim.

Loading up for the trip home that particular evening was nothing less than chaos. The heavens had opened up, releasing a downpour that caused excitement all around. I can't tell you which was louder - the children or the rain pounding on the roof of the van. It didn't help matters much when I tried yelling above the noise to get everyone settled down to get a head count.

In fact, things continued to get worse. Trying not to get soaked while I counted my cargo, I leaned into the open passenger side door, holding onto the frame. While wanting to help, one of my precious angels accidentally slammed the front door right on my fingers! The shrill giggles and loud chatter suddenly fell silent when they saw the blood running down my knuckles. Trying to hold back my tears, I motioned for another leader to come and watch over the children while I went back inside the church to nurse my wounds and calm my emotions.

Finally, on the road and headed home, the conversation was calm and low. I'm so thankful they couldn't hear the conversation in my heart and mind! "Lord", I said, "Why do I keep doing this? All I feel like is a glorified babysitter! Is this even worth it?!"

As I continued my one-person pity party, an old hymn gently began to play in the background of my mind: "It will be worth it all, when we see Jesus; life's trials will seem so small, when we see Christ." I was so ashamed!

The Lord had clearly given me an opportunity to be a light in the lives of these precious children and I had failed. Not knowing any of their situations, I may have been the only Jesus they would ever see! In that moment I asked the Lord to forgive my selfish heart and let me try again! And, He has...many times over!

"Then they brought the little children to Him, that He might touch them; but the disciples rebuked those who brought them. But when Jesus saw it, He was greatly displeased and said to them, "Let the little children come to Me and do not forbid them; for such is the kingdom of God..." And He took them up in His arms, laid His hands on them, and blessed them." Mark 10: 13-14, 16 (NKJV)

Yes, I've already signed up for VBS this year - and no, I won't be driving the van. Those days have passed. However, you can find me in the kitchen fixing the meals and handing out the cookies and Kool-Aid! Why? Because the Lord may bring just one child that needs the Jesus who lives in me. "It will be worth it all!"

It Will Be Worth It All, written by Esther Kerr Rushtoi

The Toothbrush

My toothbrush disappeared! I know it sounds ridiculous, but it's true! How on earth could one grown woman, who seems to be fairly sane and held together, misplace something as simple as this?! I assure you that my house is not a mess, and my bathroom is tidy!

Being a creature of habit, I always brush my teeth while standing in the same spot, and then I put everything away in the same cabinet! Even funnier is the fact, that I did not lose the toothpaste! And before you ask, "Yes, I did look in the cabinet—more than once!"

What a comfort to know that God always knows where I am. Psalms 139 tells me there is never a time when He doesn't see or hear me. He knows exactly where I am, every second of every day. He is watching over me, and nothing can move me out of His sight or pluck me out of His hand. It doesn't matter if I'm on the mountaintop or in a deep, dark valley; because of the blood of Christ, in Him, I am secure.

He also knows my thoughts and actions before I've carried them out. This also makes me painfully aware that His ever-watchful eye sees me when I sin, which then brings consequences. Because He loves me with a love that I cannot comprehend, His discipline can seem hard. "No discipline seems enjoyable at the time, but painful. Later on, however, it yields the peaceful fruit of righteousness to those who have been trained by it." Hebrews 12: 6,11 (CSV) I'm so thankful!

All of the above is true for every Born-Again Child of God. Even when He seems to be silent, He is there, always watching His own. If you're in doubt, I encourage you to read the entire chapter of Psalms 139. He promises to never leave or forsake you. (Deuteronomy 31:6, Hebrews 13:5)

By the end of the week, I had given up hope of ever finding my toothbrush. I'm thankful for the multi-pack I purchased a while back, and I'm quite sure my husband appreciated it, too.

Not being one to give up, I went back to check the cabinet one more time, and sure enough, off to the side, there it lay. What a comfort to know that I'm never misplaced by my Savior.

Lord, thank you for your constant watch over me. No matter the situation, You are there. "Such knowledge is too wonderful for me; it is high, I cannot attain it." - Psalms 139:6 (CSB) By faith, however, I believe.

Snowstorm of the Year

The forecast was certain as the snowstorm of the year was headed our way! Experts were all in agreement that we would be receiving some of the largest amounts of the white powder that had fallen in years! The beautiful - yet messy - event was to last for an entire day and into the evening, leaving a perfect white blanket across the open fields. With the pantry well stocked and excitement in my soul, I was prepared! However, my enthusiasm was short lived. By early afternoon, those beautiful flakes stopped falling as an unexpected "dry spot" entered the area. As it moved through, my dreams of being snowed in exited along with it. Yes, we received a nice little snow event, but it wasn't the big one all the experts were calling for. I then began to smile at the Lord.

Job 37: 5-18 (NKJV) says:
"God thunders marvelously with His voice; He does great things which we cannot comprehend. For He says to the snow, 'Fall on the earth'; Likewise to the gentle rain and the heavy rain Of His strength. He seals the hand of every man, that all men may know His work. The beasts go into their dens and remain in their lairs. From the chamber of the south comes the whirlwind, and cold from the scattering winds of the north. By the breath of God ice is given, and the broad waters are frozen. Also with moisture He saturates the thick clouds; He scattered His bright clouds. And they swirl about, being turned by His guidance, That they may do whatever He commands them on the face of the whole earth. He causes it to come, whether by correction, or for His land, or for mercy.

Listen to this, O Job; Stand still and consider the wonderful works of God. Do you know when God dispatches them and causes the light of His cloud to shine? Do you know how the clouds are balanced, those wondrous works of Him who is perfect in knowledge? Why are your garments hot, when He quiets the earth by the south wind? With Him, have you spread out the skies, strong as a cast metal mirror?" Not only did I smile, I laughed out loud. It is God who tells the snow when and where to fall.

As I peered out my window the next morning, God's intricate handiwork was on display. Individual snowflakes, too numerous to count, covered the ground. Each one, uniquely crafted and then woven together, had created quite a masterpiece! I stood in awe.

Man tried his best to determine just how much snow we would receive and where it would land, but after it was all said and done, God had the final say. This reminds me of another day that's been forecasted. As Jesus ascended into Heaven, He promised that one day He would return to take us home. Ever since, man has tried to predict when that day would be. However, Jesus clearly said that, "no man knows the day or the hour" (Matthew 24:36-51). So dear reader, my question to you: Are you prepared and watching with excitement?

Final Thought from My Heart

Since God called me to public ministry so many years ago, there has been one word that would never leave me alone: Transparency. So much of my life has always been an open book, yet I must admit to you that that's not always easy! Just like you, there are some things I would rather just keep between Jesus and me!

Throughout these pages though, I pray that's what you've seen. I've tried to be as real as I could be! I'm no super Christian! Life can be hard at times and so often I have failed miserably. But you see, there was always hope! His name is Jesus! His arms of grace and mercy are always open.

If you're still searching for this hope and needing peace, I assure you, dear reader, it's available to you as well. Simply call out the name of Jesus and ask Him to save you, and He will!!

Romans 10:9-11says, If you confess with your mouth the Lord Jesus and believe in your heart that God has raised Him from the dead, you will be saved! For with the heart one believes to righteousness and with the mouth confession is made to salvation. For the scripture says, "Whoever believes on Him will not be put to shame."

From the bottom of my heart, you are so loved and appreciated!

~ Cheri Taylor

Made in the USA
Coppell, TX
14 November 2025